**Embracing a New Normal
& Why We Can't Go Back!**

**Embracing a New Normal
& Why We Can't Go Back!**

By Christy Brubaker

Spiritual Reset: Embracing a New Normal & Why We Can't Go Back!
Copyright @ 2020 by Christy Brubaker
All rights reserved.

No part of this book may be reproduced in any form or by any electronic or mechanical means, including information storage and retrieval systems, without permission in writing from the author.

Scripture quotations marked (AMP) taken from the Amplified® Bible, Copyright © 2015 by The Lockman Foundation. Used by permission.

Scripture quotations marked (AMPC) taken from the Amplified® Bible Classic, Copyright © 1954, 1958, 1962, 1964, 1965, 1987 by The Lockman Foundation. Used by permission.

Scripture marked (MSG) taken from *The Message*. Copyright © 1993, 1994, 1995, 1996, 2000, 2001, 2002. Used by permission of NavPress Publishing Group.

Scripture marked (NIV) taken from THE HOLY BIBLE, NEW INTERNATIONAL VERSION®, NIV® Copyright © 1973, 1978, 1984, 2011 by Biblica, Inc.™ Used by permission. All rights reserved worldwide.

Scripture marked (NKJV) taken from the New King James Version®. Copyright © 1982 by Thomas Nelson, Inc. Used by permission. All rights reserved.

Scripture quotations marked (NLT) are taken from the Holy Bible, New Living Translation, copyright © 1996, 2004, 2007 by Tyndale House Foundation. Used by permission of Tyndale House Publishers, Inc., Carol Stream, IL 60188. All rights reserved.

Scripture quotations marked (TPT) are from The Passion Translation®. Copyright © 2017, 2018 by Passion & Fire Ministries, Inc. Used by permission. All rights reserved. ThePassionTranslation.com.

ISBN: 978-0-578-73678-5 (Paperback)
Religion / Christian Living / Personal Growth
Religion / Christian Living / Spiritual Growth

Dedicated to:

My Lord and Savior, Jesus Christ

Table of Contents

Introduction 9

Chapter 1: From Striving to Abiding 17

Chapter 2: From Distraction to Devotion 27

Chapter 3: From Rushing to Waiting 37

Chapter 4: From Worry to Worship 47

Chapter 5: From Complacency to Urgency 59

Chapter 6: From Assumption to Appreciation 71

Chapter 7: From Temporal to Eternal 81

Afterword 91

Introduction

We are in the midst of a global pandemic. A highly contagious virus that originated in China has spread like wildfire throughout the entire world. At this writing, over half a million people have lost their lives as confirmed cases exceed 10 million. Wow! Sounds like something out of the newest Sci-Fi-thriller, doesn't it? Public schools are shut down, forcing teachers and administrators to create lesson plans and teach their kids virtually. Federal and state authorities have issued "shelter-in-place" orders and "social-distancing" guidelines, previously unfamiliar terms that have suddenly become the norm for our societies. Health care workers and all food supply workers are on the "front lines" of this battle against this deadly respiratory virus. These, along with other "essential" workers are our heroes, as they daily risk being exposed to the virus. The economy has taken a major blow and unemployment has skyrocketed as so many "non-essential" workers have lost their jobs. Fortunately, many are able to hold on to their jobs by working from home.

Sporting events are non-existent. Movie theaters, salons, barber shops, malls, dine-in restaurants are closed, though many take-out and drive-thrus remain open. Many other organizations and businesses where people congregate are closed as well. This includes houses of worship. A shocking statement, indeed.

Our church buildings are closed. I get the mandatory precautions; stay home, stop the spread, save lives. I also understand that the shutdown of our churches is not an attack on our religious freedom but is a matter of public health and safety. Here in North Carolina, I read the executive order issued by our governor that actually lists houses of worship as "essential," which is encouraging. However, there is a mandate of no gatherings of more than 10 people, which covers just about all of our churches. (Before the completion of this book, thankfully, houses of worship were removed from the ban on public gatherings, although many churches decided to stay closed or gradually open back up). One thing is for certain: even with church buildings being closed, the *Church* has been very active!

Everything we see happening right now, in the year 2020, is unprecedented. We have never been here before. We are in uncharted waters, but we are all in the same boat, which actually brings us some solace and semblance of unity. Even more significantly comforting is the fact that none of this has come as a surprise to our great God. He was not caught off guard, nor is He trying to scramble, frantically trying to find a way out of this mess. On the contrary, He is The Way. He is The Truth. He is The Life. Everything that we will ever need is found in Him. Our gaze should be so fixed on Him during this time that nothing and nobody can move us.

In fact, this should be our posture at ALL times, not just during times of crisis. That's FAITH. To declare, "God, I trust You. I look to You. I don't know what's going on. I don't understand what's going on. But I KNOW that You do. So, I ask for Your will to be accomplished. Your plans and purposes to be executed as You see necessary." We can pray this way when we know and realize that one of the attributes of God is His Sovereignty. He is ultimately in control of the universe that He created. I would rather put my trust in He who is perfect, who knows the end from the beginning, whose thoughts are higher than my thoughts and whose ways are higher than my ways, than to trust in finite, fickle, and flawed man.

Now, let's understand two things. First of all, we have a crisis in our world that has brought about many radical changes in how we live and do life. Secondly, in moving forward, how we respond to those changes will have a significant impact on the spiritual climate of those who follow Christ. In other words, will the Bride of Christ be reawakened, refreshed, renewed, reignited, realigned and therefore be made READY for His soon return? Or, will the Bride of Christ go back to the doldrums of complacency, excessive busyness, old lovers, misaligned priorities and dead religion? Will we revert or reset? Will we revert to our old ways, or will we allow the Spirit of God to reset our lives in a way that makes us watchful, while working and waiting for the sudden, yet fully expected, return of the Bridegroom for His Bride?

I have heard statements like, "I can't wait for things to go back to normal!" Or some say, "I wish things would go back to the way they were before." A booming economy is awesome. Record unemployment is amazing. But go back? God forbid.

"Normal" wasn't working; not for the church, and therefore, not for the world. It is my prayer (and the prayer of many others), that followers of Jesus Christ take this time that we were forced into a season of rest, to become more intimately acquainted with His Spirit, dive deeper into the love letter of His Word, and receive the revelation and preparation that we need for the end time harvest of souls. In effect, that we embrace a NEW normal. If you are reading this and you do not have a personal relationship with the Lord Jesus Christ, then I am confident you will discover the blessed Hope in Him revealed throughout these pages. You will then have a choice to make: repent and believe the Good News of the Gospel of Jesus Christ resulting in eternal life with Him, or reject Him and be forever separated from Him in the lake of fire that was prepared for the devil and his demons.

With the onset of this virus, COVID-19, we are more keenly aware of the birth pangs Jesus mentions in Matthew 24:6-7:

> "And you will hear of wars and rumors of wars. See that you are not troubled; for all these things must come to pass, but the end is not yet. For nation will rise against nation, and kingdom against kingdom. And there will be famines, pestilences, and earthquakes in various places. All these are the beginning of sorrows" (NKJV).

A pestilence is a raging epidemic; a contagious, devastating plague. That Scripture just became more real to us here in the United States of America. May the Lord continue to open our spiritual eyes to what must take place before we reach our eternal state. May He grant us wisdom for every test, strength for every battle, power for every attack, peace for every storm, endurance for every trial, and His everlasting love to sustain us through it all.

The following chapters will reveal some truths about where we were ("we" referring to the Church) and the hopeful status of where we could be moving forward from COVID-19. I believe it's God's heart for us. I believe it because it's in His Word and I believe His Word. You may be surprised. You may be offended. You may be self-righteous. You may be humbled. May we all repent. Every great move of God throughout history involved a season of repentance. To repent is to turn from our sin and turn to God. We are on the precipice of a paradigm shift in the Kingdom of God on this earth. Will you embrace the reset? I'm ready to jump. Are you?

Chapter 1

From Striving to Abiding

"He who says he abides in Him ought himself also to walk just as He walked."
1 John 2:6 (NKJV)

You've heard of "The American Dream." Lots of money, a nice job, status, a nice house, vehicles, success, fame, notoriety—everything a person could want on this earth. From early on, we are taught to climb that ladder of success until we reach "the top." Everyone has probably got their own version of what that looks like, but our pursuit of it looks the same. It's called *striving*. Dictionary.com defines striving as: *"to exert oneself vigorously; try hard"* (Random House). Sound at all familiar? Sometimes we camouflage it as "just wanting to support my family," or "I just want my kids to have things I didn't have," or "I just want to be the best that I can be." There's this drive to strive that, if not calibrated, can lead to a crash: in our family, our marriage, our business, or even our physical or mental health.

Don't misunderstand. We shouldn't be passive and certainly not lazy. The Bible warns against these attitudes. But does the end goal of "The American Dream" really sound all that great when looking through the lens of eternity?

> *"For what will it profit a man if he gains the whole world, and loses his own soul?"*
> Mark 8:36 (NKJV)

You see, it's not that obtaining any of these things mentioned is, in and of itself, bad. It's more a matter of priorities. There are times in our lives that we are so zoned-in on the striving for things in the natural that we neglect our spiritual health. Our personal relationship with God should be the number one priority in our lives. Period. In Matthew 6:33, Jesus tells us to, *"Seek the Kingdom of God above all else, and live righteously, and he will give you everything you need."* In other words, if HE has first place in my heart and in my life, He will provide for my needs. Not necessarily all my wants, but all my needs.

I am convinced that many Believers don't intentionally misalign their priorities; however, when we recognize it, we need to swiftly make the necessary corrections. What would that look like? It may mean cutting out the overtime at work, cutting up the credit cards that are increasing your debt, limiting your travel or extra-curricular activities, decreasing your time in front of the TV, computer or smartphone, understanding that your child does not have to be involved in every sport or club at school, or fill in the blank as it pertains to your life. The Holy Spirit is our Guide. Don't ignore the gentle promptings and convicting urges from Him. Allow Him full access to your heart and your home, with permission to rearrange as He desires.

And don't think just because *your* striving is ministry-related that this doesn't apply to you. You can be doing the work of the Lord and still neglect your relationship with Him. I remember a time early in my walk with the Lord that I got caught up in the striving. I felt like I had to say "yes" to everything I was asked to do in the church, step in when there was "no one else to do it," and work really hard to "prove" myself to Him. What I failed to fully understand was that His love for me was not dependent on my performance or my people-pleasing, but solely on the work of Jesus Christ on the cross on my behalf. The more I pursued my relationship with Him, the more He revealed His love for me. It was then that what had previously felt like "duty," became delight, and what felt like "obligation," turned to devotion.

We have become accustomed and all too well-acquainted with striving. Yet with the coronavirus hitting our nation, our striving has come to a sudden, screeching halt. But, unfortunately, it wasn't by choice, but by necessity. Everything basically has been shut down in order to stop the spread of this virus. So, as we await the starting bell to resume our busy lives, we come to a fork in the road. Will we continue on the path of striving, or may I suggest the other path, the one called "abiding?"

The word "abide" is an, "Old English word signifying progressively to 'await,' 'remain,' 'lodge,' 'sojourn,' 'dwell,' 'continue,' 'endure;'..." (Orr). In

John's Gospel, we see a beautiful picture of abiding given by Jesus to His followers:

> *"I am the vine, you are the branches. He who ABIDES in Me, and I in him, bears much fruit; for without Me you can do nothing"* (John 15:5, NKJV, emphasis added).

We are not just connected; we remain, we dwell, even live (as The Amplified Bible states) in Him, and Him in each of us. This is a union, a bond, that produces fruit. What is that fruit? Anything that comes from Him will come from us. Compassion, service, generosity, humility. Galatians 5:22-23 lists the fruit of the Spirit. It's worth taking note of since it is His Spirit that actually dwells inside of us:

> *"But the fruit of the Spirit produces this kind of fruit in our lives: love, joy, peace, patience, kindness, goodness, faithfulness, gentleness, and self-control..."* (NLT).

Notice how Jesus stated that we wouldn't just bear fruit, but *much* fruit. This shouldn't be surprising when we remember that we serve a God of abundance, of more than enough; the God of the overflow. Who wouldn't want to abide in Him?

Additionally, we must realize that without Him, we can do nothing. You may say, "Oh, I can do plenty!" Listen to this Commentary regarding the phrase "we can do nothing."

> ...for without me ye can do nothing; nothing that is spiritually good; no, not anything at all, be it little or great, easy or difficult to be performed; cannot think a good thought, speak a good word, or do a good action; can neither begin one, nor, when it is begun, perfect it. Nothing is to be done "without Christ"; without his Spirit, grace, strength, and presence; or as "separate from" him. Were it possible for the branches that are truly in him, to be removed from him, they could bring forth no fruits of good works, any more than a branch separated from the vine can bring forth grapes; so that all the fruitfulness of a believer is to be ascribed to Christ, and his grace, and not to the free will and power of man (Gill's Exposition of the Entire Bible).

Apart from Him, we are spiritually dead; therefore, unable to do anything of spiritual or eternal significance. I spent years of my life trying to fill a void, an emptiness, with the things of the world. Once I surrendered to Him, I knew that His goodness would in turn cause me to respond through my good works: now, not because I had to, but because I wanted to. It was and is a way of expressing my love and gratitude towards Him.

Abiding does not mean that we just hang out with Jesus on Sundays for an hour or two or connect with Him when we're going through a rough time. It means we are continually and consistently united with Him in such a way that we are never separated. Jesus further explains the analogy in verses 9-10 of John 15:

> *"As the Father loved Me, I also have loved you; abide in my love. If you keep My commandments, you will abide in My love, just as I have kept My Father's commandments and abide in His love"* (NKJV).

It's His love that remains forever. And He set the example for us by demonstrating in the flesh a life of obedience to the Father.

Abiding is a lifestyle. We dwell with Him. That's a good place to be. Many Believers have been quoting and clinging to Psalm 91 during this very difficult time of COVID-19. You may be very familiar with this Psalm because of some other difficulty you have had to walk through in your life. It is comforting and assuring to know from the first verse that *"He who* dwells *in the secret place of the Most High shall* abide *under the shadow of the Almighty"* (NKJV, emphasis added). The secret place is that place of refuge, that place of safety in God. As the Psalmist goes on to say in verse 4, *"He shall cover you with His feathers, and under His wings you shall take refuge."* What a beautiful picture of the nurturing and protecting embrace of the Father for His children, just as an eagle cares for her young.

Perhaps you are reading this, and you feel a tug, a desire, to have something like what has just been described. Maybe you have had a life of dead religion, rituals, and routine, void of any intimacy with the God who fashioned you in the womb. Some of you may have wandered off from the relationship you once had with Him. Still others may not have ever been introduced to Him. Whatever the case, take a moment and choose to repent and believe the Good News of the Gospel.

> *"For God so loved the world, that He gave His only begotten Son, that whoever believes in Him should not perish, but have everlasting life"* (John 3:16, NKJV).

If you trust in Him for salvation, you are born again, and His Spirit has come to live inside of you! Listen for His voice, as He will speak to your heart and transform your life!

As we come to the end of this chapter, I will ask you to search your heart and determine whether you are ready for a reset. We have been given a moment to reflect, to self-examine. Will you allow the Holy Spirit to make the necessary adjustments to cease from striving and live your life abiding in Christ? It is in Him that you will live life to the fullest and produce much fruit!

Chapter 2

From Distraction to Devotion

"All the believers devoted themselves to the apostles' teaching, and to fellowship, and to sharing in meals (including the Lord's Supper), and to prayer."
Acts 2:42 NLT

Distractions abound daily in our lives. There is such an abundance of them that a book could be written with vivid descriptions of how we can easily, yes, easily become distracted. Our kids get distracted from their homework or their chores by things like TV, tablets, iPads, smartphones, or video games. Adults get distracted from their tasks by the very same devices. My husband gets distracted while driving if he sees some deer off in the tree line.

Others can get distracted while driving by eating, changing the radio station, or using their cell phones. These are just a few examples of external distractions.

Then we have internal distractions. Maybe as you're reading a book, possibly this one, your mind has wandered off to something you forgot at the grocery store, some job you forgot to complete at work, or maybe you were distracted by the drool you felt coming down your chin because you fell asleep! You could be at work and get distracted from your job with thoughts of what someone said to you (or how they said it), or with thoughts of what you need to try and get done once you get home. I think you get the picture. We are overwhelmed with distractions.

Now, we must also understand that we have an enemy, the adversary, the devil, who wants to steal, kill and destroy us. He knows that he can't get many of us to stray by the more obvious ways that he keeps the world ensnared; like with partying or fornication (although some may fall for this). And he, knowing that we allow different things to capture our attention and our focus from one activity to another, will use this as a subtle tool to cause distractions in our spiritual lives. When it comes to the things of God, we must be diligent and intentional. The prophet Isaiah says it so well:

> *"Because the Sovereign Lord helps me, I will not be disgraced. Therefore, I have set my face like a stone, determined to do his will"* (Isaiah 50:7 NLT).

He would not be moved; not by distractions or ridicule or anything that man could do to him.

You may be familiar with the following scenarios. You sit down to read your Bible and one of two things happen (or maybe both): your child needs help with some "crisis," like a scratch that necessitates a Band-aid, or your phone starts blowing up with texts or notifications from email or social media. Or maybe you finally have some time to pray and get alone with God, and as soon as you sit down and start praying, you start to fall asleep because you have been so busy doing other things that now you are exhausted. (We'll be discussing busyness a little later). What about when you finally get the family to church (late) and your worship leader is trying to get you and everyone else engaged in praising and worshipping our great God, and your mind starts to think on where you're going to go eat after church because you just don't feel like cooking today? Or the Pastor is bringing a Word that the Lord wants the Body to hear that will strengthen and encourage, and you start mentally going through your calendar for the week and totally miss what the Spirit is saying to you at that moment?

Can we pause for a moment and realize that distractions in our lives have kept us from God's best for us? They can keep us from maturing in our walk with the Lord, keeping us stagnant and unproductive in any meaningful way for the Kingdom. Many distractions have been removed during this pandemic that we are experiencing right now. Maybe in retrospect we can now see that some of the things that have been removed were indeed distractions. What an opportune time we have right now to set our faces like flint (a stone) and determine in our hearts to avoid the enemy's snare of distraction that has often captured us unaware and, instead, pursue a life of devotion to the One who is worthy of our attention and our affections.

Devotion can be defined as an "earnest attachment to a cause, person, etc.," or a "profound dedication, esp. to religion; consecration" (Random House Kerneman Webster's College Dictionary). Oh, that we may "attach" ourselves to the cause of Christ and consecrate our lives in service to Him! Jesus Himself demonstrated devotion to His Father when He was but 12 years old. The story is in Luke when Joseph and Mary took Him to Jerusalem as required for Passover. The Scripture states that Jesus, *"lingered behind in Jerusalem"* (Luke 2:43, NKJV). His parents did not even realize that they had left Him, and after three days had passed, they found Him in the temple, amazing the religious teachers with His understanding and questions. When they scolded Him, Jesus stated in verse 49, *"Why did you seek Me? Did you not know that I must be about My Father's business?"* Notice the word "must." The work of the Father was paramount. May we learn from this that devotion to the Father doesn't result after years of spiritual maturity, but is necessary from the inception of our journey with Him.

    It's a matter of deciding to go ALL IN. Allow me to share just a couple of examples from God's Word, as it is our manual for life, our guide to Truth and THE FINAL AUTHORITY (as my mentor, Pastor Judy Jacobs Tuttle always says)! I can't help but recall the prophet Daniel. He was taken from his country and his people into Babylonian captivity (you can read about him in the book named after him). He did not allow the customs and practices of this pagan nation to be *distractions* from his dedication and commitment to Almighty God. He didn't eat the food or partake of the drinks offered to him. For the record, he wasn't alone. Three other young men were just as committed: Shadrach, Meshach, and Abed-Nego. Because of their unwavering determination to go all in with God, He gave them all, *"knowledge, and skill in all literature and wisdom; and Daniel had understanding in all visions and dreams"* (Daniel 1:17 NKJV). In fact, King Nebuchadnezzar found them to be *ten times better* than the magicians and astrologers under his rule (verse 20)!

There was a time when Shadrach, Meshach and Abed-Nego refused to bow to a golden, graven image of Nebuchadnezzar specifically because of their devotion to God. They ended up being thrown into a fiery furnace that had been heated seven times hotter, but not before declaring that their God was able to deliver them from the furnace, and, *"... if not, let it be known to you, O king, that we do not serve your gods, nor will we worship the gold image which you have set up"* (Daniel 3:18 NKJV). And as they were in the fire, a fourth Man appeared (that would be Jesus) in the midst of them, and they were unharmed! I love how the Scripture states that when the three men came out, the people saw, *"the men on whose bodies the fire had no power; the hair of their head was not singed nor were their garments affected, and the smell of fire was not on them"* (verse 27). What an amazing God we serve! He is still able to deliver you, sustain you, be with you and protect you in the midst of whatever fiery trial you might be facing!

God showed Daniel great favor and supernatural protection as a result of his wholehearted devotion. He was given a position of authority and was given dreams and visions not only of his present time, but of the end times! Unfortunately, his consistent devotion to God got him thrown into a den of lions under the rule of King Darius. Daniel always knelt down on his knees three times a day to pray and give thanks to God. Some jealous leaders, who despised him, tricked the king (who actually liked Daniel) into signing a decree that no one prays to any god for 30 days or they will be thrown into a den of lions. After being thrown into the den, God sent an angel to shut the mouths of the lions and Daniel was unharmed! You can find this story in Daniel 6. My friend, we are not even aware of all the times that God dispatches his angels on our behalf or intervenes in our situations and struggles as a direct result of our devotion to Him!

We can't leave the topic of devotion without looking at the New Testament church! The book of Acts chronicles the activities and the events surrounding the followers of Jesus after His ascension back to Heaven. There is an excellent and timeless model for Believers demonstrated in Acts 2:42-47 that we can glean from today. It's a true formula for success as it relates to the Kingdom of God. What could be more important than that?

"All the believers devoted themselves to the apostles' teaching, and to fellowship, and to sharing in meals (including the Lord's Supper), and to prayer. A deep sense of awe came over them all, and the apostles performed many miraculous signs and wonders. And all the believers met together in one place and shared everything they had. They sold their property and possessions and shared the money with

those in need. They worshiped together at the Temple each day, met in homes for the Lord's Supper, and shared their meals with great joy and generosity—all the while praising God and enjoying the goodwill of all the people. And each day the Lord added to their fellowship those who were being saved" (NLT, emphasis added).

Wow! Their relationship with God and one another wasn't defined by just a casual getting together when it was at their convenience or because there wasn't anything else to do at the moment. No, they were *devoted*. Sold out. All in. They had seen the Messiah in the flesh. They saw Him dead. They saw Him resurrected. They saw Him ascend into the heavens. They tarried (waited) and received the baptism in the Holy Spirit on the day of Pentecost. In short, their lives were radically and permanently transformed!

How would you characterize your relationship with Jesus? Is it casual or committed? Is it shallow or is it deep? Has He radically transformed your life? What is keeping you from a life of devotion to Him? He tells us in Luke's Gospel to count the cost before choosing to follow Him. Salvation is free but following Him will cost you. I hope you will discover the joy in devoting yourself to the Word of God, to fellowship with other believers, and to prayer. When we do this, corporately, as one body, the Kingdom of God grows exponentially! COVID-19 has claimed many lives prematurely. As we ponder the brevity of life and discover our purpose in God's ultimate plan, let us choose to move forward (from *any* crisis) in devotion and not be drawn back into the distractions that have hindered us from walking in our calling, and finally, our destiny.

Chapter 3

From Rushing to Waiting

"Be still, and know that I am God;
I will be exalted among the nations,
I will be exalted in the earth!"
Psalms 46:10 NKJV

If we could have a dollar for every time we have all made the statement, "I just didn't have time," or, "There's just not enough hours in the day," we would all be rich. We rush, rush, rush, trying to utilize every second of every hour of every day to accomplish our plans or "to-do" list for the day. There's just so much to do and not enough time to do it, right? I feel you. I do. I've been there. Overcommitting, making sure our kids are involved in community or school activities, working more hours than our bodies are equipped to handle, trying to make time for family and extended family get-togethers, trying to find time to exercise, clean, cook, and not to mention rushing to check the boxes on our spiritual disciplines. I prayed in the car on the way to work (check the prayer box). I read the devotional verse on my desk at work (check the Bible reading box). I made it to church two Sundays this month and even squeezed in one Wednesday night service (check the fellowship box). Let's not be prideful enough to think that we're doing God any favors. Do you think He wants ANY leftovers from your busyness?

    I know this seems a little harsh. "I'm trying the best that I can," is a statement I used to say to God a lot. Many times, we don't recognize the devastation our busyness has caused until it's almost too late. Our physical health begins to deteriorate. Our marriage is on the rocks. Our kids are distant, feeling neglected and unloved. Most importantly, our relationship with God is affected. We begin to feel like He is far away; however, He is not the one who moved. If we're honest, our relationship with God has looked more like spiritual prostitution rather than consecration, with us coming to Him when we have a need to be met rather than coming to Him just to "be." None of us set out to be so busy—rushing here, there, and everywhere—but by the mercy of God, He has allowed things to happen in order for us to reflect and see the constant state of busyness that many of us were in prior to this pandemic.

When I think of rushing and being busy, I am reminded of the story of Mary and Martha. You may be familiar with this passage, but it is worth revisiting. Read it slowly. Notice the emphasis:

> "Now while they were on their way, it occurred that Jesus entered a certain village, and a woman named Martha received and welcomed Him into her house. And she had a sister named Mary, who seated herself at the Lord's feet and was listening to His teaching. But Martha [overly occupied and too busy] was distracted with much serving; and she came up to Him and said, "Lord, is it nothing to You that my sister has left me to serve alone? Tell her then to help me [to lend a hand and do her part along with

me]!" But the Lord replied to her by saying, "Martha, Martha, you are anxious and troubled about many things; There is need of only one or but a few things. Mary has chosen the good portion [that which is to her advantage], which shall not be taken away from her" (Luke 10:38-42 AMPC, emphasis added).

The problem isn't that what Martha was doing was wrong. Someone has to cook, someone has to prepare, someone has to serve. However, in this particular moment, Martha chose the preparations over the Presence. She was consumed by many things instead of the One thing. Which is more advantageous? Mary made the better choice. The ability to choose is a powerful gift. God knew that every generation from that time on would need this example of waiting over rushing. Waiting at the feet of Jesus, lingering on His every Word, versus rushing about, too busy to stop and hear what the Master has to say.

Once a person is on that treadmill of rush, rush, rush, it's hard to get off. You may feel overwhelmed and even trapped. You must take bold, decisive steps to make the necessary corrections. How do you do that? Are you ready? It's in the power of your pen (or in the power of your fingertips). YOU are the one that controls your calendar, not the other way around. Quite frankly, I grow weary of hearing, "But I have to do this..." or "I've got to..."

YOU have control over those 30 (or 31) white boxes each month, just as YOU have control of the 1,440 minutes in each day. The Lord never intended for us to fill every space on our calendar (He's removed from time anyway); on the contrary, He wants us to love Him with ALL our heart, mind, soul and strength. Loving Him this passionately and wholeheartedly would require ample space on our calendars, don't you agree? He is either first, or He's not. He either reigns on the throne of your heart, or he doesn't. We live in a fast-paced, constantly moving society. As Believers, let us determine to live counter-culturally, avoiding the hustle and the hurry. Now let's turn our attention to the "better" thing: waiting.

Pausing, lingering, tarrying, waiting, resting. Just reading those words sounds refreshing, doesn't it? Putting it into practice, however, is somewhat challenging. This is something we must be very intentional about. It will not come naturally or easily, because most of us feel that to be productive and/or effective is to be busy. But in God's Kingdom, waiting on Him is one of the wisest things we could do. There are so many beautiful Scriptures that portray the benefits of waiting on Him, so to share a few of them here is most appropriate, and I hope, helpful.

> *"The Lord is good to those who wait hopefully and expectantly for Him, to those who seek Him..."* (Lamentations 3:25 AMPC).

> *"But those who wait on the Lord shall renew their strength; They shall mount up with wings like eagles, They shall run and not be weary, They shall walk and not faint"* (Isaiah 40:31 NKJV).

> *"Here's what I've learned through it all: Don't give up; don't be impatient; be entwined as one with the Lord. Be brave and courageous, and never lose hope. Yes, keep on waiting—for he will never disappoint you"* (Psalms 27:14 TPT).

> "I waited patiently for the Lord; he turned to me and heard my cry. He lifted me out of the slimy pit, out of the mud and mire; he set my feet on a rock and gave me a firm place to stand" (Psalms 40:1-2 NIV).

Wow! We receive so much from just waiting on the Lord! We receive strength, His goodness. He never disappoints; He hears, and responds! Need I remind you that the enemy does not want you receiving anything from Almighty God, so he will try to cause you to move ahead—it's this tool called impatience—but doing so in your own strength will only cause you to make the wrong choices (or even the right choice at the wrong time) and possibly have to reap some unpleasant consequences. Wait on God. Let Him lead. Linger in His Presence. Until. Until you have peace, wisdom, comfort, assurance, a Word, a confirmation. These things do not usually come quickly, but nothing worth having ever does!

Jesus gave these instructions to His followers just before His ascension:

> "Behold, I send the Promise of My Father upon you; but tarry in the city of Jerusalem

until you are endued with power from on high" (Luke 24:29 NKJV).

This promise of the Holy Spirit is repeated in the first chapter of Acts and here Jesus also tells them:

"But you shall receive power when the Holy Spirit has come upon you; and you shall be witnesses to Me in Jerusalem, and in all Judea and Samaria, and to the end of the earth" (Acts 1:8 NKJV).

Now let's put this in perspective. These followers had families. They had jobs. They had debts. They had other obligations. If this scenario played out today, I could just hear the excuses as to why "ain't nobody got time for that!" Sure, many did walk away. After all, Jesus was seen by more than 500 of His followers after the resurrection. Only 120 ended up assembling in the Upper Room to WAIT. Perhaps the 120 knew that they couldn't do what Jesus had commissioned them to do without the help of the promised Holy Spirit. Oh, how we need that same help today! I believe we can all testify that it was worth the waiting. They didn't know if it would be two days, ten, or twenty! All they knew was that they had to wait on God!

In this short life that we are blessed with, may we learn that there's regret in the rush but reward in the wait. Practice being still in His Presence. That takes time, but doesn't any meaningful and intimate relationship? Be intentional about making room for Him, and I mean every day, not just Sundays. I am positive that what He has to say is far more important than what your calendar says.

Chapter 4

From Worry to Worship

"There is no room in love for fear. Well-formed love banishes fear. Since fear is crippling, a fearful life—fear of death, fear of judgment—is one not yet fully formed in love."
1 John 4:18 MSG

It's quite overwhelming when you consider all the things we tend to worry about. We worry about our children. We worry about their education, what kind of influence their friends will have on them. We worry about their safety, their health, their choices. And even when they're grown, we have similar concerns. With our jobs, we worry about getting along with our co-workers, getting enough hours to take care of our bills, doing our jobs correctly and effectively or meeting deadlines. We worry about our finances; whether we will be able to pay all the bills, put money in savings, take that vacation, or buy something we really need. We worry about our security. We wonder if we're safe at night; will someone break in? Are we safe walking to our vehicle at the mall, or who will take care of us when we are old? In our relationships, we worry about getting married, or not getting married, we worry if that person will like us, love us, reject us or accept us. We worry if our marriage will last, or if our strained relationships with our children will improve. We worry about our future, like what we will do when we retire, whether we'll have good health, or money, or if we will we be alone. We worry a lot about things that may not even happen—the "what-if" worries. For example, "What if that storm comes this way? What am I going to do? What if a tree falls on my house?" Or maybe, "What if my boss (or teacher) doesn't like my presentation? What if I fail?" Could you admit to any of these worries listed above? I think we can all confess "guilty" at some point.

Worry, anxiety, and stress are all synonymous with fear. They are all ways that fear, being afraid, will manifest itself in our lives. Because our Creator knows us so well, He has a lot to say about fear and worry in His Word. If we will take these truths and really apply them to our lives, we won't succumb to this particular tool of the enemy. Yes, fear (worry) is yet another way that the enemy will try to keep your focus off of the hope that you have in Christ; the assurance you have in Him, and the peace that you have full access to as a born again believer in Him! Jesus gives a beautiful illustration about worry in Luke 12:

> *"Then, turning to his disciples, Jesus said, "That is why I tell you not to worry about everyday life—whether you have enough food to eat or enough clothes to wear. For life is more than food, and your body more than clothing. Look at the ravens. They don't plant or harvest or store food in barns, for God feeds them. And you are far more valuable to him than any birds! Can all your worries add a single moment to your life? And if worry can't accomplish a little thing like that, what's the use of worrying over bigger things?*

Look at the lilies and how they grow. They don't work or make their clothing, yet Solomon in all his glory was not dressed as beautifully as they are. And if God cares so wonderfully for flowers that are here today and thrown into the fire tomorrow, he will certainly care for you. Why do you have so little faith? And don't be concerned about what to eat and what to drink. Don't worry about such things. These things dominate the thoughts of unbelievers all over the world, but your Father already knows your needs. Seek the Kingdom of God above all else, and he will give you everything you need. So don't be afraid, little flock. For it gives your Father great happiness to give you the Kingdom. Sell your possessions and give to those in need. This will store up treasure for you in heaven! And the purses of heaven never get old or develop holes. Your treasure will be safe; no thief can steal it and no moth can destroy it. Wherever your treasure is, there the desires of your heart will also be" (Luke 12:22-34 NLT).

How comforting this passage is! He sees. He knows. He cares. Trust Him. Focus on Him. He knows exactly what you need. He is not removed from your struggle nor is He unconcerned about it. Our fears and worries should not dominate our thoughts as children of the Most High God. If we allow it to consume us, our physical health will decline, and our soul (the mind, will, emotions) will be in turmoil.

Part of our problem is that we tend to cling to what is comfortable, and at times, fear seems more familiar to us than faith. For example, when Jesus came to the disciples walking on the water, how many stepped out in faith and got out of the boat? Only one, Peter. The others remained inside the boat! I love Paul's encouragement to young Timothy:

> *"For God has not given us a spirit of fear, but of power and of love and of a sound mind"* (2 Timothy 1:7 NKJV).

We must understand that fear does not come from God. It's quite the opposite, as you see in this verse. He gives us power to overcome the enemy, love that casts out the fear, and a sound mind. The Amplified Bible describes the "sound mind" as a "calm and well-balanced mind and discipline and self-control."

In other words, God desires that we have peace. The following Scripture is life-changing if we truly apply it to our lives:

"Don't worry about anything; instead, pray about everything. Tell God what you need, and thank Him for all He has done. Then you will experience God's peace, which exceeds anything we can understand. His peace will guard your hearts and minds as you live in Christ Jesus" (Philippians 4:6-7 NKJV).

May His peace reign in your heart during any test, trial, struggle, tragedy or pandemic. Jesus assures us that, *"These things I have spoken to you, that in Me you may have peace. In the world you will have tribulation; but be of good cheer, I have overcome the world"* (John 16:33 NKJV).

Just think on that for a minute. Jesus has overcome. By His sacrificial death, burial and resurrection, He has OVERCOME. What can man do to you? He has secured the victory. For all eternity.

For all people who will receive it. With this revelation, we can reject worry and respond appropriately—with our worship. May this be a profound outcome of this pandemic we are experiencing right now: that we will no longer be bound up and consumed with fear, worry and anxiety, but instead embrace a life of worship to the One who calms all our fears.

What does that look like? We must first understand what worship is *not*. Worship is not 30 minutes of singing on Sunday morning. It's not just going to church either. Worship is a *lifestyle*. It's a posture of the heart that says to God, "You are the only one worthy of my affections, my attention, my time, my talent, my treasure!" It means that we live our lives humbly surrendered to His will, obedient to His call, and loving Him above all else. I'm sure you know this, but maybe a reminder is in order: anything you place above God or anything you put before Him is an idol and you are worshipping the wrong god. Many times, we do not even realize it when we fashion other idols in our minds. We end up ignoring the promptings of the Holy Spirit inside of us that says, "Put that device down," or "This relationship is unhealthy. Cut it off now before it becomes an idol to you," or "This activity in consuming all of your extra time. Come back to your first love, Me." If we're not careful, we can worship a god of entertainment and/or sports. Any thing or any person that you devote the majority of your time to can be an idol and therefore the object of your worship. We'll explore this a little more in the last chapter.

Jesus discussed worship with the woman at the well in John 4. The encounter changed her life. As she inquired about the debated location of worship between the Jews and Samaritans, Jesus revealed that worship wasn't about a place to go but a posture to seek. It's not about a ritualistic, religious exercise but a sincere, authentic relationship with the Father. Here is Jesus' response about worship from The Message translation:

> *"Believe me, woman, the time is coming when you Samaritans will worship the Father neither here at this mountain nor there in Jerusalem. You worship guessing in the dark; we Jews worship in the clear light of day. God's way of salvation is made available through the Jews. But the time is coming—it has, in fact, come—when what*

you're called will not matter and where you go to worship will not matter. It's who you are and the way you live that count before God. Your worship must engage your spirit in the pursuit of truth. That's the kind of people the Father is out looking for: those who are simply and honestly themselves before him in their worship. God is sheer being itself—Spirit. Those who worship him must do it out of their very being, their spirits, their true selves, in adoration" (John 4:21-24 MSG).

What or who is the object of your affections and adoration? Has the Lord been in His rightful place on the throne of your heart? Maybe now is the time to reflect, repent and recommit to the only One who is worthy of worship: the One who fashioned and formed you; the One who loved you so much that He sent His Son to die for you so you could have a relationship with Him.

Your adversary—the Devil, or Satan—wants your worship. It's what he's always wanted. When Jesus was led by the Spirit into the wilderness before His earthly ministry began, Satan tried to bribe Him to worship him. Of course, that didn't work out! Could it be that he's learned throughout the centuries a more subtle way of stealing worship from the Almighty? You see, if he can get you to *worry,* then you'll neglect or reject worshipping God. If he can get your focus off of the Most High and onto your problem, your situation, your struggle, your anxiety, your circumstances, your pain or even your feelings, then worry and fear will rule in your heart and your head.

You can choose right now to leave worry behind and choose instead to worship Him: The King of kings and Lord of lords. Determine to no longer cling to that which has been so comfortable and familiar but step out and seek after the One who can calm your fears and give you rest. In other words, like the disciples, you can stay in the boat and focus on the storm or be like Peter and step out of the boat, focused on the Savior. Instead of thinking of all the things on your worry list, try recalling some of the names of God in Scripture. I can assure you that as you make a list of what He's been to you, personally, that this exercise can't help but cause you to bow down and worship Him! Just some examples that come to mind are how He is my:

- Refuge and Strength
- Strong Tower
- Deliverer
- Redeemer
- Sustainer
- Comforter
- Defender
- Savior
- Creator
- And so much more!

Let us move forward in this next season as sons and daughters committed to worshipping the Lord with our lives, wholeheartedly and intentionally so that there is no longer room for the enemy to enslave us to anxiety, fear or worry. Remember, as we acknowledge the love He has for us and reciprocate that love, there is NO ROOM for fear! If it tries to come in, it is cast OUT! What a promise!

Chapter 5

From Complacency to Urgency

> *"I know you inside and out,*
> *and find little to my liking.*
> *You're not cold, you're not hot—*
> *far better to be either cold or hot!*
> *You're stale. You're stagnant.*
> *You make me want to vomit."*
> Revelation 3:15-16 MSG

The word complacent is defined as: "Satisfied with the current situation and unconcerned with changing it, often to the point of smugness" (American Heritage). It's a hard pill to swallow that this could be the general state of the Church right now, but I believe there's overwhelming evidence that this is, in fact, the case. Nobody likes to hear anything negative. We want everything positive. However, if we don't acknowledge where we are, how can we take steps to improve? Improve in our efforts to fulfill the Great Commission? If we don't acknowledge where we are, how can we see that we need to repent and come back to our first love? Our "first love" meaning the relationship we had with Jesus when we first experienced and received His free gift of salvation.

    Let's just look at church attendance, which should be a priority among Believers. It is modeled in the book of Acts, granted the location may be varied (house church or building) and the writer of Hebrews admonishes the church to, *"not neglect our meeting together, as some are in the habit of doing, but encouraging one another- and all the more as you see the Day approaching"* (Hebrews 10:25 NLT). Thom S. Rainer states in his article, "The Number 1 Reason For the Decline in Church Attendance," that not only is church attendance declining and churches are not growing, but the main reason for the decline is, "that members attend with less frequency than they did just a few years ago" (Rainer). People are going less often. Sadly, it seems that we try to fit church into our busy schedules "if there's time" or "if there's nothing else going on," rather than adjust our schedules around a commitment to gather and worship God with other Believers and hear the Word of God. Why? Because we have become complacent. We think we have personally accomplished so much that "we're good," not needing anything and therefore not concerned about changing anything. Have we conformed to the culture rather than change it? Are we stuck in stagnation when God desires transformation? There's another word for this predicament: it's called being lukewarm.

Jesus had something to say to a lukewarm church over 2000 years ago, but it is still just as relevant and applicable to us today in 21st century America:

> "Write to Laodicea, to the Angel of the church. God's Yes, the Faithful and Accurate Witness, the First of God's creation, says: "I know you inside and out, and find little to my liking. You're not cold, you're not hot—far better to be either cold or hot! You're stale. You're stagnant. You make me want to vomit. You brag, 'I'm

rich, I've got it made, I need nothing from anyone,' oblivious that in fact you're a pitiful, blind beggar, threadbare and homeless. Here's what I want you to do: Buy your gold from me, gold that's been through the refiner's fire. Then you'll be rich. Buy your clothes from me, clothes designed in Heaven. You've gone around half-naked long enough. And buy medicine for your eyes from me so you can see, really *see. The people I love, I call to account—prod and correct and guide so that they'll live at their best. Up on your feet, then! About face! Run after God! Look at me. I stand at the door. I knock. If you hear me call and open the door, I'll come right in and sit down to supper with you. Conquerors will sit alongside me at the head table, just as I, having conquered, took the place of honor at the side of my Father. That's my gift to the conquerors! Are your ears awake? Listen. Listen to the Wind Words, the Spirit blowing through the churches"* (Revelation 3:14-22 MSG).

Wow! Jesus sure didn't have a problem telling it like it is! But He tells us what we need to hear so we can live out God's best for us. Regardless of whether you think this was written only to the church at Laodicea or to the last "church age" that it is suggested we are currently in; this is some powerful teaching! It should give pause to each individual to self-examine, repent, and make the necessary changes with the guidance of the Holy Spirit.

Jesus always related truths to things that people could connect with and understand at the time. There were two nearby cities, Hierapolis and Colossae. Colossae was known for its refreshing cold waters that came down from the snow-covered mountains. Hierapolis was home to some hot springs, where water was hot and believed to have medicinal value. The rich city of Laodicea tried to pipe this water from both cities, but when the water finally arrived there, it was lukewarm. As I recently heard Bible Scholar and Pastor Rick Renner describe this, the water was disgusting, as minerals from the clay pipes affected the taste of the water that came in from the hot springs of Hierapolis. The point Jesus was making, as Rick Renner so clearly describes, is that His desire was for the church there at Laodicea to be either freezing cold like the refreshing, revitalizing waters of Colossae *or* boiling hot and healing as the waters from Hierapolis were. In other words, be refreshing or healing; don't be tepid, putrid and disgusting. He was describing their spiritual condition of being indifferent and in effect, leaving Jesus—the founder of the Church—*outside* of the Church. Just as the people waiting for the water to arrive spit it out because it failed to meet their expectations, so too did the Church fail to meet the expectations of Jesus. As Rick Renner goes on to say, it's not saying that He is rejecting them or that they have lost their salvation, but He is trying to bring correction and a desire for repentance.

Jesus goes on to point out that despite everything that they have, and their accomplishments, that HE should be their Source. Is He *your* Source today? Is He everything to you? We sing songs about Jesus being "everything" and how He means more than "anything else," but do we really *live* those sentiments? One of the saddest images of Jesus is the one of Him standing OUTSIDE of the church in Revelation 3:20, knocking on the door. Many don't realize that complacency has effectually removed Jesus from the Church and He is standing there, pounding on the door of our hearts to allow Him back in to take His rightful place; which is exactly what happened to the church at Laodicea. This isn't a verse for the unsaved. It's a Word for the saved!

Paul lays out for us in 2 Timothy how many people would behave in the last days and how they would have *"a form of godliness but denying it's power..."* (2 Timothy 3:5). The New Living Translation puts it this way: *"They will act religious, but they will reject the power that could make them godly."* The power is rejected or denied because we have fallen into complacency. We don't know what it means to seek God "until He comes." We just want the clock to strike twelve so we can leave and go on about our busy day. As our lives have slowed down during this pandemic (or any future crisis), it is my prayer for you that God is rekindling the cold embers of complacency and igniting fresh fire into your spirit man. Fire consumes. It engulfs. It causes to burn. May our passion be reignited for HIM and shift us from complacency to urgency.

The Lord is portrayed in Scripture as a Refiner. Malachi 3:2-3 describes Him like a *"blazing fire that refines metal..."* and *"like a refiner of silver, burning away the dross"* (Malachi 3:2-3 NLT). The dross represents all the impurities of our lives that rise to the top and are then removed. It's the fire of God that purifies us. He is also a *"consuming fire"* (Hebrews 12:29). It's the fire that Jeremiah felt *"shut up in his bones"* so that he could not give up (Jeremiah 20:9). It's the fire that the followers of Jesus felt burning in their hearts on the road to Emmaus as He ministered to them after His resurrection. It's the fire that fell on the 120 in the upper room on the day of Pentecost. It's the same fire that will burn in us as we seek after Him. It's the same fire that will keep us fervent and passionate for the things of God, and therefore a sense of urgency for others to have that same kind of relationship with Him.

There was a time I got sick and didn't have medical insurance, so I went to Urgent Care. I needed treatment and I needed it immediately. The Doctor prescribed some medication for me that quickly eased my symptoms. There's a time-sensitive disease that many people have that its symptoms are called sins and the only cure is Jesus. In *your* sphere of influence, there are many people who do not have a personal relationship with Him; they have not been born again. Since we don't know exactly when He is coming back (as the Word clearly teaches), there should be a consistent sense of urgency to carry out the Great Commission—that is, to make disciples. I'm sure no one reading this would want anyone to die and go to hell, being forever separated from the One who gave them life. Of course, the enemy doesn't want us keeping these thoughts at the forefront of our mission and purpose on this earth, so he will use many of the things we have discussed to distract us from advancing the Kingdom by leading others to Christ. There's a compelling story in Luke's Gospel that Jesus tells about a servant going out and inviting guests to his master's banquet:

> *"Jesus replied: "A certain man was preparing a great banquet and invited many guests. At the time of the banquet he sent his servant to tell those who had been invited, 'Come, for everything is now ready.' But they all alike began to make excuses. The first said, 'I have just bought a field, and I must go and see it. Please excuse me.' Another said, 'I have just bought five yoke of oxen, and I'm on my way to try them out. Please excuse me.' Still*

another said, 'I just got married, so I can't come.' The servant came back and reported this to his master. Then the owner of the house became angry and ordered his servant, 'Go out quickly into the streets and alleys of the town and bring in the poor, the crippled, the blind and the lame.' 'Sir,' the servant said, 'what you ordered has been done, but there is still room.' Then the master told his servant, 'Go out to the roads and country lanes and compel them to come in, so that my house will be full. I tell you, not one of those who were invited will get a taste of my banquet'" (Luke 14:16-24 NIV).

Those who gave excuses were indifferent, complacent, and too preoccupied to come to the banquet. The servant then *compelled* the less fortunate to come. He *urged* them to come. Could we be so on fire for Jesus that we live out our lives with the same sense of urgency that this servant had? As we have experienced a great loss of human life from a virus, let us recognize the urgency to sharing the Good News of the Gospel, and as Paul teaches: *"Make the most of every opportunity in these evil days"* (Ephesians 5:16). No longer will we allow complacency to be palatable. As we, *"taste and see that the Lord is good..."* (Psalm 34:8), let us continually compel others to come and feast at His table!

Chapter 6

From Assumption to Appreciation

Everything in the world is about to be wrapped up, so take nothing for granted. Stay wide-awake in prayer. Most of all, love each other as if your life depended on it. Love makes up for practically anything. Be quick to give a meal to the hungry, a bed to the homeless—cheerfully. Be generous with the different things God gave you, passing them around so all get in on it: if words, let it be God's words; if help, let it be God's hearty help. That way, God's bright presence will be evident in everything through Jesus, and he'll get all the credit as the One mighty in everything—
encores to the end of time. Oh, yes!
1 Peter 4:7-11 MSG

I think there's one huge takeaway that everyone can get from this pandemic: we assume way too much! We assume that our kids will be able to hop on a bus and be instructed at school all day. We assume that we'll be able to go to our jobs after the weekend. We assume that we can make it to the basketball tournament, meet our friends for dinner at a restaurant, or go work out at the gym. We assume we can go get our hair done or take the kids to the park. Let's not forget our families that we assume we will gather with on Easter, or Mother's Day, or perhaps a wedding or a funeral. And, of course, we make an assumption that the church we attend will be open. We assume, that when we feel like going, the doors will be open. We have made so many assumptions.

Another way of stating this is to acknowledge that we take things for granted. We do not hold certain privileges (and rights) with the care and gratitude that we should. Can we not see now that ANY thing; whether a human life, a right, a privilege, a job, a possession, an activity, can be taken away immediately—at any moment? There's one who probably knows this reality better than anyone. His name was Job. There's a book in the Bible named after him. He had it all. Wealth, health, family, land, livestock. He was the epitome of success. But most importantly, he had a relationship with God. When God allowed Satan to cause Job to suffer by stripping away his children, his servants, livestock, his cattle, his sheep, and eventually striking his own health, Job makes a profound statement that we can all learn from in any time of loss:

> *"And he said: 'Naked I came from my mother's womb, And naked shall I return there. The Lord gave, and the Lord has taken away; Blessed be the name of the Lord.' In all this Job did not sin nor charge God with wrong"* (Job 1:21-22 NKJV).

I'm not saying that Job took things for granted. The text says that he was a righteous and blameless man. What I am saying is that we cannot take anything for granted. We cannot just assume. God is Sovereign. He blesses His children. But He also allows things to be taken away. James Hudson Taylor, a 19th century Christian missionary to China, once stated that, "Christ is either Lord of all, or is not Lord at all" (Steer). Our confession of faith is to trust in the Sovereignty of God and His Word that tells us:

> *"And we know that all things work together for good to those who love God, to those who are the called according to His purpose"* (Romans 8:28 NKJV).

So, when things *are* suddenly taken away from us, we can have assurance that He's working things for our good and for HIS glory!

Since things that we are used to having can be taken for granted, it's also easy to end up taking for granted the things of God. When you take anything for granted, it loses its value in your eyes. Just for example, we have access to the Word of God either in print form or online. Many people groups in the world don't even have access to God's Word. When any of these people receive a Bible, they treasure it, devour it, learn from it, and obey it. On the other hand, our Bibles sit on our coffee tables and our bookshelves, and most of the time we don't even pick them up and carry them to the House of God. We also take for granted the precious time that we have to gather together corporately; coming in late or not coming at all, when it is in our power to do so.

I believe that once we recognize that we have taken so much for granted in the past and in a sense of pride have *assumed* way too much about our lives and how we live them, it will first of all cause us to repent. To say, "Lord, I am so sorry for taking so many things for granted. I am sorry for taking YOU for granted. Forgive me for assuming that all these varied things will always be a part of my life. Forgive me for treating so casually the great privilege I have to come to Your house to worship." Then, as we realize that life itself is fragile, circumstances can quickly change, possessions can be stripped away, conveniences are not always guaranteed, and how precious it is to gather together with other believers, I believe that a sense of appreciation will begin to grow and flow from our innermost being. Oh, how glorious this could be if we tenderly nurture this attitude!

Appreciation is defined as: "a feeling or expression of admiration, approval, or gratitude," or "a sensitive awareness" (Merriam-Webster). After experiencing a deadly pandemic, I believe that most of us have developed a more sensitive awareness and admiration of those working tirelessly in the health care field, those working to stock the shelves or check out your groceries at the local grocery story, and those working to protect our rights and freedoms. When you appreciate something, you are truly thankful and grateful for it. It's in the struggles and the storms that the seeds of appreciation are cultivated. You begin to look up and inward and thank God for the blessings that you once had, the ones you currently have, and the ones that you will have!

As we begin to appreciate what we have taken for granted, a change will begin to take place. Perhaps it already has. Since to appreciate something involves *expression* and not just a feeling, it will be evident in what we say, what we do, and even how we live. We will tip the restaurant server or the hairdresser more appropriately. We will thank and honor our health care workers, our governmental leaders, our military, our law enforcement. We won't complain about long lines for the things we enjoy for pleasure or entertainment. We will enjoy precious time with our parents, look forward to family gatherings and reunions, and be thankful for our spiritual leaders.

Since I am a pastor, I empathize with other pastors and church leaders who have had to work through a myriad of challenges and difficulties during this time. Trying to keep connected with the body at a time when you are prohibited from gathering causes a great deal of anguish in spirit for the one who is responsible for "tending to the flock." Many have had to adjust and learn how to use technology, audio/video platforms and find creative ways to keep their congregants engaged, while dealing with different perspectives and opinions of how the church should proceed. Not to mention the time spent in prayer and intercession for the local congregation, meeting any physical needs, and hearing from God a rhema Word that will encourage, equip and strengthen the Body during such a difficult season. I pause here to just say, "Thank you!"

Now, can we just turn our attention to the ONE who is worthy of the utmost appreciation, our Lord and Savior, Jesus Christ? May our hearts never take for granted the blood that was shed, the sacrifice that was made, the debt that was paid for you and for me on the cross. The apostle Paul admonishes us in 1 Corinthians 15:57:

"But thank God! He gives us victory over sin and death through our Lord Jesus Christ" (NLT).

Our appreciation to Him can be expressed in many different ways—through communing with Him in prayer, serving Him wholeheartedly and joyfully in the local church or community ministry, reading, studying and meditating on His Word, obeying His Word, using our Spiritual Gifts to equip the body, giving back to Him with tithes and offerings, singing praises to Him, worshipping Him in spirit and in truth, and sharing the Gospel and our testimony with those who do not know Him. The book of Psalms is an excellent source of verbal appreciation to God. It would be beneficial to read some of it every single day! Just one example is:

"Enter his gates with thanksgiving; go into his courts with praise. Give thanks to him and praise his name" (Psalm 100:4 NLT).

The first century church changed the culture. The Gospel spread like wildfire as people turned to Christ and walked in obedience to Him. People abandoned their powerless, lifeless idols and encountered the power of the Holy Spirit. They spoke with new tongues, they cast out demons, they healed the sick, raised the dead. Jesus tells us in Mark 16:17 just before His ascension that *"these signs will follow those who believe..."* (NKJV). As we move forward from assumption to appreciation, may His power be manifested as we express our appreciation to Him and FOR His glory in the earth!

Chapter 7

From Temporal to Eternal

*"Long ago you laid the foundation of
the earth and made
the heavens with your hands.
They will perish, but you remain forever;
they will wear out like old clothing.
You will change them like a
garment and discard them.
But you are always the same; you will live forever."*
Psalm 102:25-27 NLT

The last piece of embracing a new normal can be summed up in one word: focus. What or who has your gaze? What or who are your affections for? What or who consumes your thoughts, your time, your attention, your finances? If we're honest, there are times when our focus is on what we see right in front of us. Our focus is on what can satisfy us in the moment, even though it's short-lived and often unfulfilling. God created so many wonderful things for us to enjoy and observe. However, what we must understand is that everything we SEE with our eyes is *temporary*. We only have a short amount of time to bring the lost to Christ and to advance His Kingdom on this earth. Therefore, we must hold loosely the temporary in order to cling to that which is eternal. We have to fix our focus, that sometimes gets fuzzy because of the enemy or because of a lax in our own spiritual disciplines. To "fix our focus" can also be described as "setting your mind." It's an intentional disruption of whatever is trying to capture your gaze. The Apostle Paul said to:

> *"Set your mind and keep focused habitually on the things above [the heavenly things], not on things that are on the earth [which have only temporal value.] For you died [to this world], and your [new, real] life is hidden with Christ in God"* (Colossians 3:2-3 AMP).

There is an old saying that we should "not be so heavenly-minded that you are no earthly good." I don't think this is even possible. It is precisely because of being heavenly-minded that we are empowered and emboldened to live a life of going about doing good in the earth. That's what was said about Jesus: *"He went about doing good..."* (Acts 10:38, AMPC).

Additionally, sometimes our focus can be not on a person or a thing, but on the troubles of this life. We are certainly going through some troubles (globally) right now! Again, Paul gives us some insight into these troubles:

"For our present troubles are small and won't last very long. Yet they produce for us a glory that vastly outweighs them and will last forever! So we don't look at the troubles we can see now; rather, we fix our gaze on things that cannot be seen. For the things we see now will soon be gone, but the things we cannot see will last forever" (2 Corinthians 4:17-18 NLT).

What a revelation! What a promise! It's when we fix our gaze on what (and WHO) can't be seen that we are better able to handle what can be seen. Knowing that there's something more real than what I can see with my natural eyes, gives me the ability to not be so attached and fixated to the temporary but be entranced by the Lover of my soul; the One who is preparing a place for me right now!

Let's address the issue of *why* things that are temporal can become our focus. It's because many times the temporal things can become idols. We don't intentionally set out to do this, but it happens, nevertheless. As believers, we are IN the world, but not OF the world. The things that capture the attention of the world (and are thus "idols"), should not capture our attention. For example, the Israelites, *"...mingled with the [idolatrous] nations and learned their ways, and served their idols, which became a [dreadful] snare to them,"* and *"...in this way they became unclean in their practices; they played the prostitute in their own deeds [by giving their worship, which belongs to God alone, to other "gods"]"* (Psalm 106:35-36, 39 AMP, emphasis added). When we lie in bed with the world, we develop a spirit of prostitution—committing adultery with God by dividing our affections between an outward profession of love to Him, but an inward confession of lust to the world. Let me be clear: ANY THING or ANYONE that you place before God is the object of your worship; and therefore, is an idol.

God must be first, as mentioned previously. This is a truth that must be taught to our children and our grandchildren. If it's not, then the generations after us will turn to other idols. They will embrace and enthrone the temporary (momentary, fleeting) pleasures and miss out on the eternal ones! Eternity is a very long time! Listen to what happened with the children of Israel and let's determine that history will NOT repeat itself on *our* watch:

> *"After that generation died, another generation grew up who did not acknowledge the Lord or remember the mighty things he had done for Israel. The Israelites did evil in the Lord's sight and served the images of Baal. They abandoned the Lord, the God of their ancestors, who had brought them out of Egypt. They went after other gods, worshipping the gods of*

the people around them. And they angered the Lord" (Judges 2:10-12 NLT).

The gods of today may not be golden or graven images, but they are fashioned in the forms of entertainment, sports, addictions, etc. But why *settle?* Why settle for the earthly, temporary pleasures when God has unimaginable, eternal pleasures for His sons and daughters? Psalm 16:11 declares:

"You make known to me the path of life; you will fill me with joy in your presence, with eternal pleasures at your right hand" (NIV).

Doesn't that make you want to know *more?* What does God have to say about eternity?

Daniel had a vision concerning the return of Christ and His Kingdom. Which, by the way, all the fulfilled prophecies that we see in the Bible is profound and compelling evidence that the rest of the prophecies WILL unfold! Listen to what Daniel saw:

"In my vision at night I looked, and there before me was one like a son of man, coming with the clouds of heaven. He approached the Ancient of Days and was led into his presence. He was given authority, glory and sovereign power; all nations and peoples of every language worshiped him. His dominion is an everlasting dominion that will not pass away, and his kingdom is one that will never be destroyed" (Daniel 7:13-14 NIV).

Disappointment and destruction abound in the fallen world in which we live. Yet, we have an opportunity to share the love of Jesus and tell about what He *has* done, *is* doing, and what He *will* do! We have hope (a confident expectation) about His soon return, so let us live our lives in light of eternity, with great anticipation that John spoke of:

"Dear friends, we are already God's children, but he has not yet shown us what we will be like when Christ appears. But we do know that we will be like him, for we will see him as he really is. And all who have

> *this eager expectation will keep themselves pure, just as he is pure"* (1 John 3:2-3 NLT).

Do you have this eager expectation? May we search our hearts and ask the Lord to purify us, cleanse us, forgive us, of any temporal thing that has caused us to be guilty of idolatry. Especially during times like these, may we see that when the earth and everything in it is shaken, that which remains is the unshakeable, eternal and all-powerful God, His Word, and His Kingdom!

As we are living in the last of the last days, there are many who live to gratify the desires of the flesh and mock those who walk in the Spirit. They walk in darkness, their eyes veiled because they have not received the free gift of salvation through Jesus Christ. Peter warns us about this:

> *"Above all, you must understand that in the last days mockers will multiply, chasing after their evil desires. They will say, "So what about this promise of his coming? Our ancestors are dead and buried, yet everything is still the same as it was since from the beginning of time until now""*
> (2 Peter 3:3-4, TPT).

These "mockers" are lost and in desperate need of a Savior. Maybe you or someone you know are one of these. It's not too late. In this same chapter of 2 Peter, he goes on to explain that God is waiting because He is not willing for anyone to die in their sins. He wants everyone to know His Son and trust in Him for salvation. It's His mercy that delays His return, yet only He knows when the end will come. It is my prayer that the Bride of Christ lives the abundant life that He came to give, while shifting her focus from the temporal to the eternal. This life we are given is like a vapor; so brief in light of all eternity. As we have been reminded about the brevity of life by those taken so suddenly by tragedy, sickness, or disease, may we rejoice with each day we are given and embrace the new normal of a refocused, renewed, realigned, refreshed and revived spirit, soul and body: a total RESET—a reset that remains the default setting—no matter what kind of disruption (or virus) the enemy tries to cause. Please don't go *back*. What lies ahead is greater than what lies behind. God's Word is a guarantee of that!

Afterword

It's amazing to see the kindness of people demonstrated during this pandemic. There are businesses, churches and non-profits donating meals to families and children. There are businesses modifying their production of products to include face masks, Personal Protective Equipment, and even hand sanitizer. There are others delivering meals or organizing parades to encourage first responders and our health care workers.

Some other noteworthy observations: I have seen many posts on Social Media of families doing activities together, cooking together, and making music together. I have seen many photos taken of God's creation, like a flower, a bird, a tree, a sunset, clouds, and more. Not that photos like these haven't been taken in the past, but there has definitely been an increase in these types of photos as our busyness has dissipated over a period of months that so many have been "quarantined."

It's been a joy to see social media flooded with churches ministering to their congregations online, via Facebook Live or some other streaming service. The Gospel has gone out to more people in more places as pastors embrace the use of technology in order to stay connected. This pandemic has certainly pushed many who are in ministry out of their comfort zones, stretching them and sparking creativity in thinking of ways to stay engaged with the body.

Although many have lost their lives due to this virus, there are also some who have received miraculous healing. There have been many stories published and reported of people being on ventilators, at the point of death, and they surprisingly and miraculously experience a complete recovery. These stories bring glory to God.

There have also been photos published of stores that have empty shelves where the Bibles were located! People are hungry for more. People are searching for answers. People are thinking about death and dying and therefore thinking more about their souls. The Lord will speak to them through His Word and bring transformation to the one who's heart is open to Him.

Surely, we will all recognize the positive and inspiring changes that have taken place during the pandemic of COVID-19. I have heard it said that it takes 21 days to form a habit. We've journeyed through this for longer than that. Could it be that the body of Christ has formed such refreshing and deeply satisfying new habits that going back to the way things were before is not even an option? Could we be so invigorated with new life and freedom from chains that had us bound, that we embrace the new normal before us—the "normal" that was God's intention all along? Why would we go back to bondage? The Lord has opened our eyes. Let us be repentant, humble ourselves before Him and accept the reset that has been activated by the Lord's mercy, grace and love for His people who had temporarily deviated from the default setting of His wonderful plan for their lives!

If I may conclude with an exception to the statement in the subtitle of this book that "we can't go back," there is *one* thing that would be most beneficial for us to go back to, and that is, our *first love,* as mentioned briefly in chapter 5. There's a song by Maverick City Music that has these powerful lyrics:

"When the storm is out on the ocean, and the violent wind gets to blowing, oh, take me back, back, all the way back. Oh, take me back to my first love."

That first love is *Jesus.* His Word teaches us that we are continually being transformed into His image:

> *"So all of us who have had that veil removed can see and reflect the glory of the Lord. And the Lord-who is the Spirit- makes us more and more like him as we are changed into his glorious image"* (2 Corinthians 3:18 NLT).

We love for the Holy Spirit to encourage us, strengthen us, empower us and affirm us; but, we also must *allow* Him to discipline us, purify us, correct wrong mindsets, and reveal any sin in our lives so we can repent and go to that *next level* of glory. The *new normal* IS the *next level!* Are you ready? Let's GO!

Works Cited

American Heritage Dictionary of the English Language, Fifth Edition. Houghton Mifflin Harcourt Publishing Company. 2016. www.thefreedictionary.com/complacent. Accessed 11 May 2020.

"Appreciation." *Merriam-Webster.com Dictionary.* Merriam-Webster. www.merriam-webster.com/dictionary/appreciation. Accessed 24 May 2020.

Gills Exposition of the Entire Bible. Bible Hub: Search, Read, Study the Bible in Many Languages. 2004-2020. www.biblehub.com/commentaries/john/15-5.htm. Accessed 20 April 2020.

Maverick City Music. Lyrics to "Take Me Back." Genius Media Group Inc. 18 October 2019. genius.com/Maverick-city-music-take-me-back-lyrics. Accessed 18 June 2020.

Orr, James. M.A., D.D. General Editor. "Entry for 'ABIDE'." *International Standard Bible Encyclopedia.* 1915. www.biblestudytools.com/dictionary/abide/. Accessed 20 April 2020.

Rainer, Thom S. "The Number 1 Reason For the Decline in Church Attendance." *Facts and Trends,* 17 December 2018. www.factsandtrends.net/2018/12/17/the-number-1-reason-for-the-decline-in-church-attendance/. Accessed 13 May 2020.

Random House Kernerman Webster's College Dictionary. Random House, Inc. 1991. www.thefreedictionary.com/devotion. Accessed 20 April 2020.

Random House Unabridged Dictionary. Random House Inc. 2020. www.dictionary.com/browse/striving. Accessed 19 April 2020.

Steer, Roger. "Hudson Taylor: Lessons in Discipleship." *OMF International*, p.34, 1995. www.en.m.wikiquote.org/wiki/James.Hudson.Taylor. Accessed 24 May 2020.

www.ingramcontent.com/pod-product-compliance
Lightning Source LLC
Chambersburg PA
CBHW071410290426
44108CB00014B/1758